# The Process of
# Drawing Animals
## Activity Book

activibooks for kids
Coloring, Drawing & Activity Books For Children

# INSTRUCTIONS FOR DRAWING:

THIS HOW-TO DRAWING BOOK CONSISTS OF IMAGES THAT ARE PLACED ON GRIDS. THERE IS AN EMPTY DRAWING BOX WITH GRIDS THAT WILL SERVE AS YOUR PRACTICE SPACE. TO COPY EACH IMAGE, DRAW PARTS OF THE IMAGE PER GRID AND PUT THEM ON THE BLANK GRIDS. SOUNDS DIFFICULT? NOT REALLY. TRY IT FIRST!

IT'S OKAY IF YOU DON'T COPY THE IMAGE PERFECTLY. AFTER ALL, DRAWING IS ABOUT THE EXPRESSION OF YOUR PERCEPTION AS WELL AS YOUR HAND STRENGTH AND CONTROL.

WHEN YOU'VE COPIED THE IMAGE, GO AHEAD AND COLOR IT NEXT! WE'RE EXCITED TO SEE WHAT YOU CAN DO!

# DRAW THE IMAGE

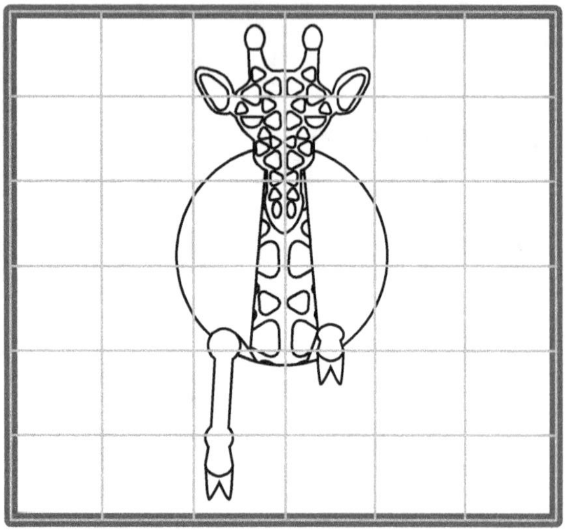

# DRAW THE IMAGE

# DRAW
## THE IMAGE

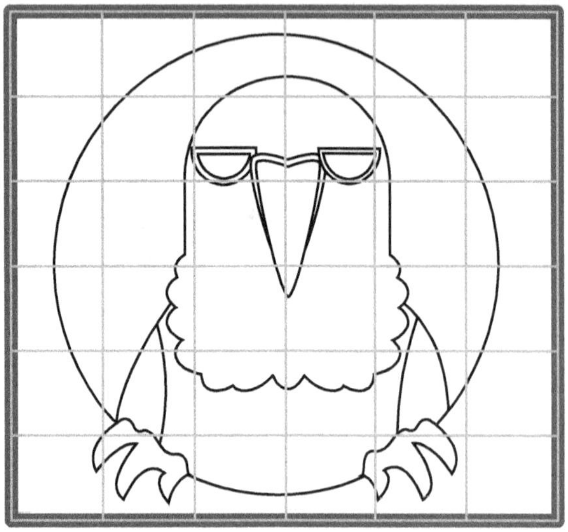

# DRAW THE IMAGE

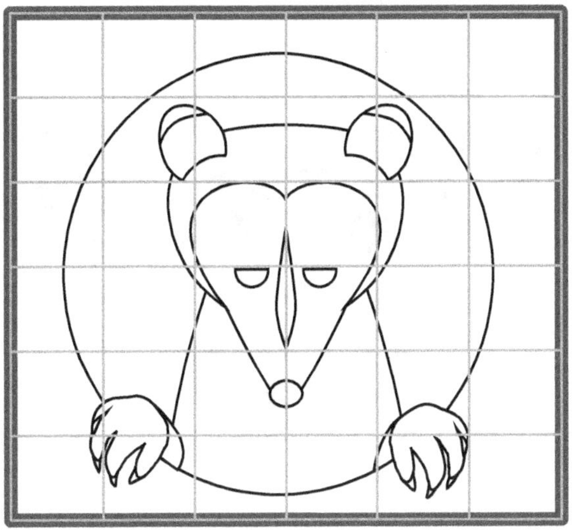

# DRAW
## THE IMAGE

# DRAW THE IMAGE

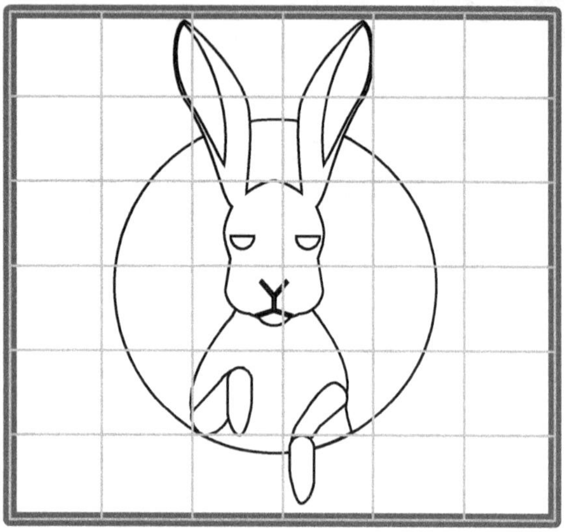

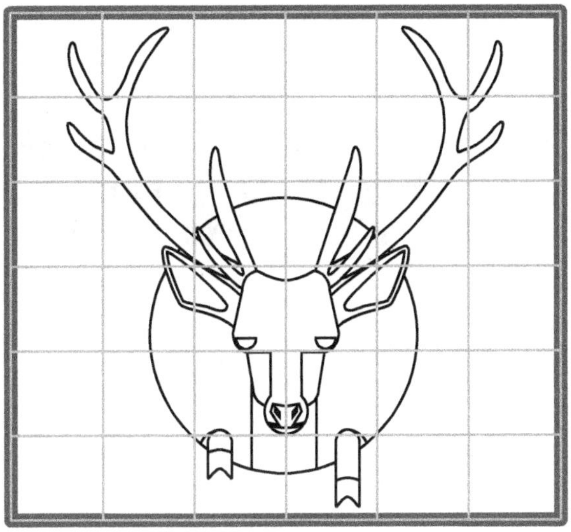

# DRAW THE IMAGE

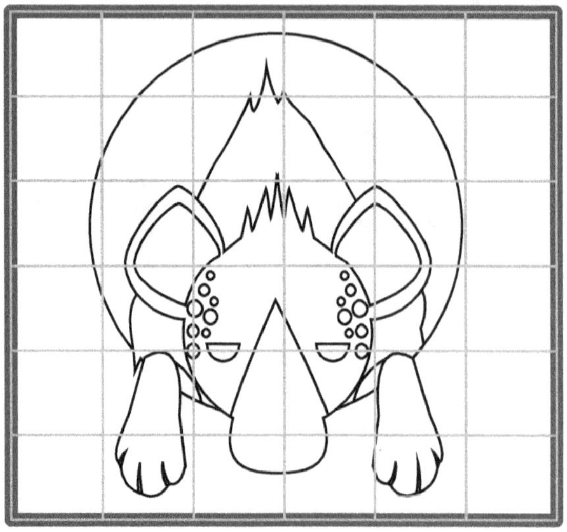

# DRAW THE IMAGE

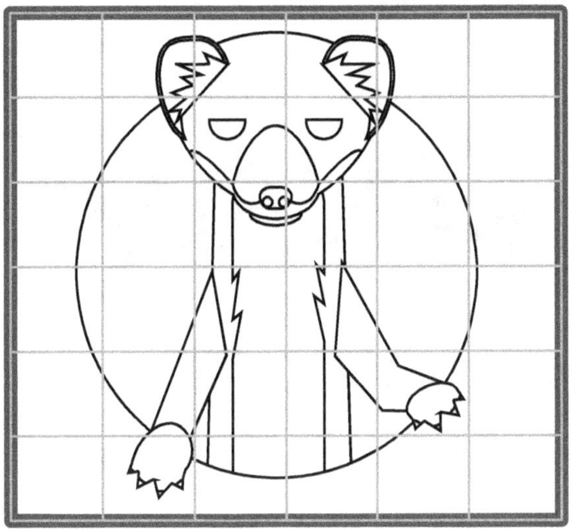

# DRAW THE IMAGE

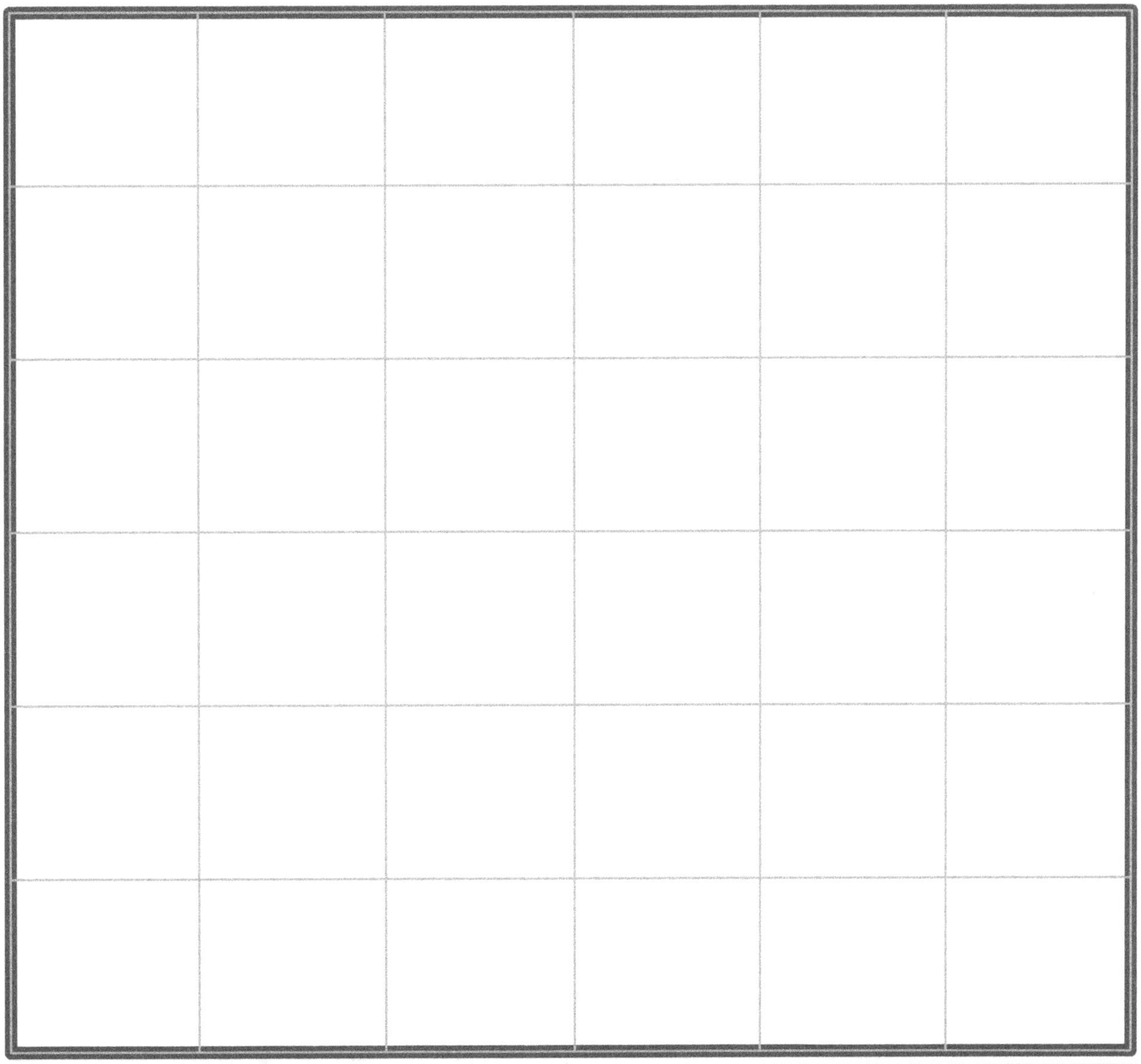

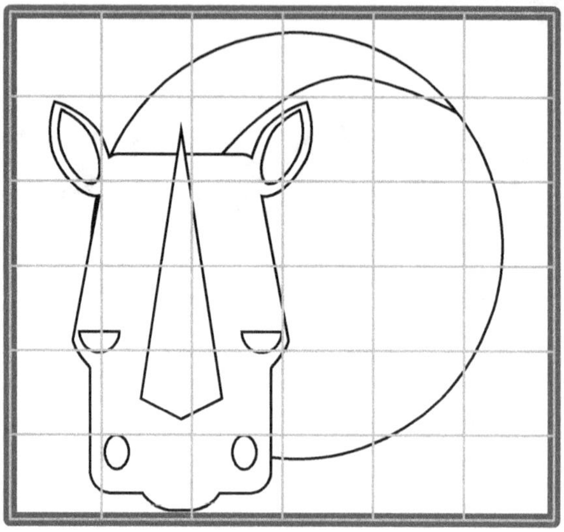

# DRAW
## THE IMAGE

# DRAW
## THE IMAGE

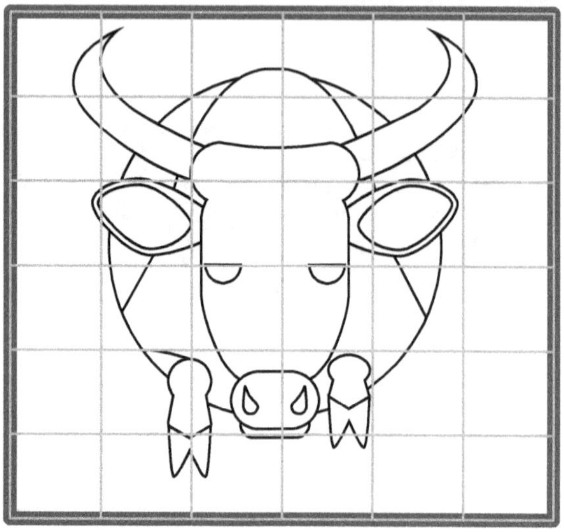

# DRAW
## THE IMAGE

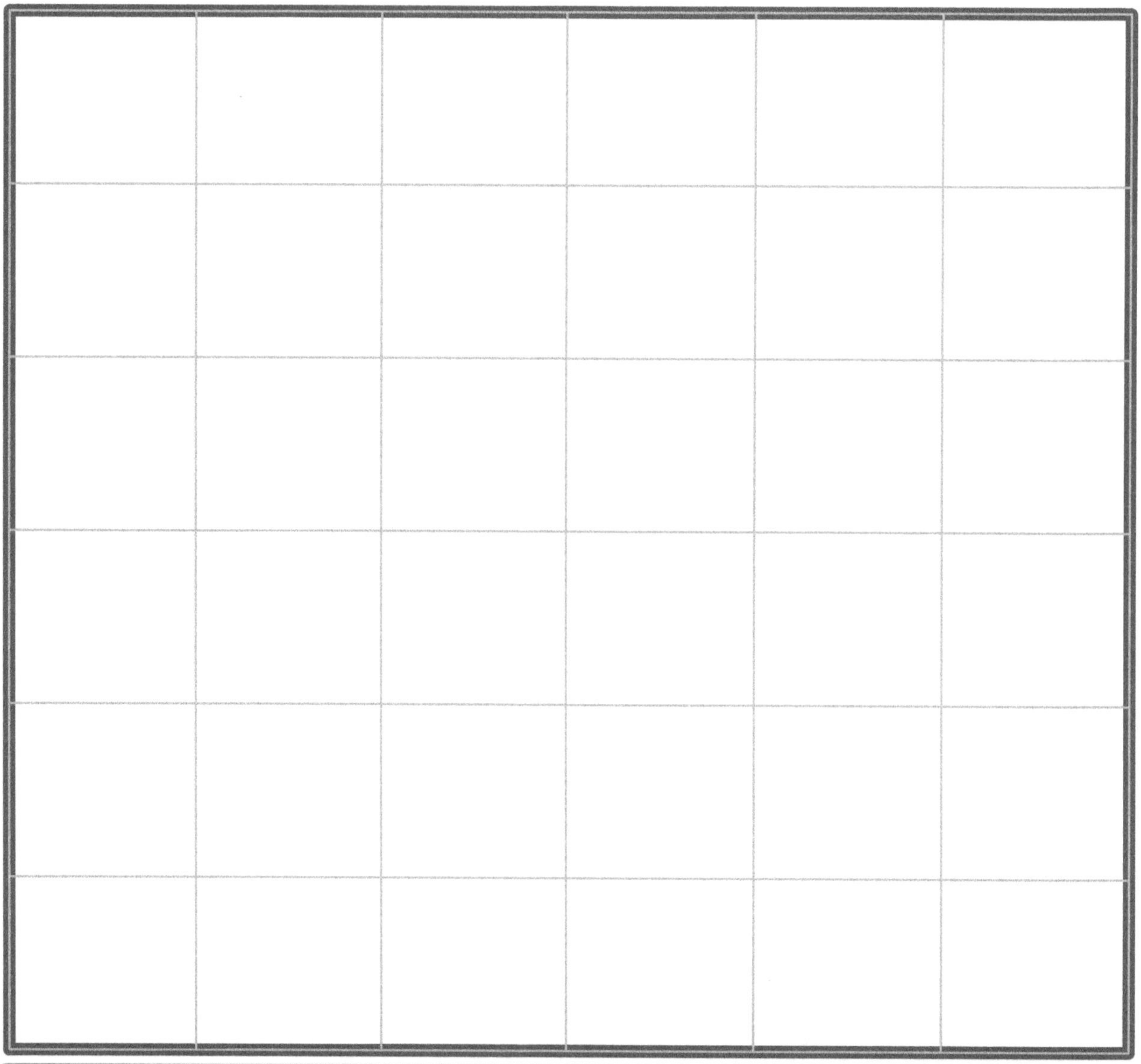

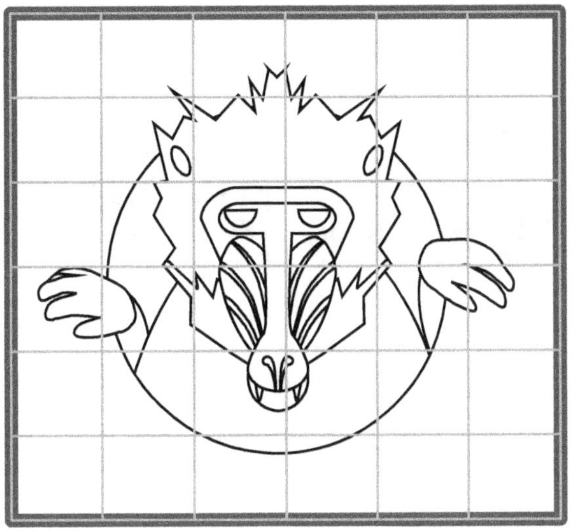

# DRAW THE IMAGE

# DRAW
## THE IMAGE

# DRAW
## THE IMAGE

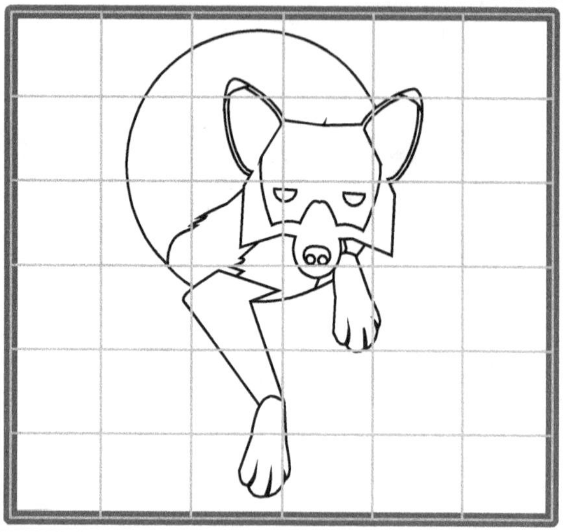

# DRAW THE IMAGE

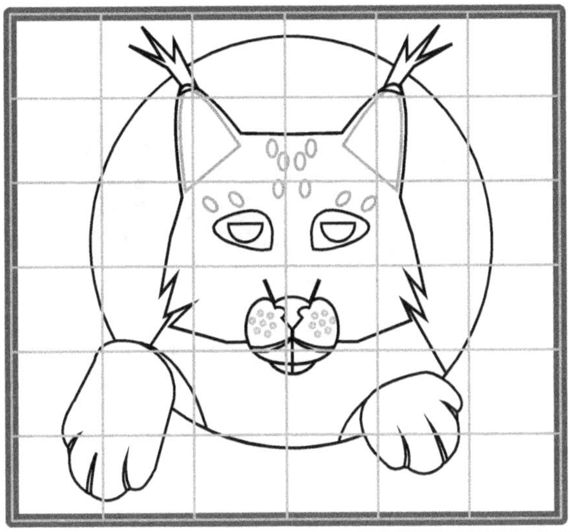

# DRAW
## THE IMAGE

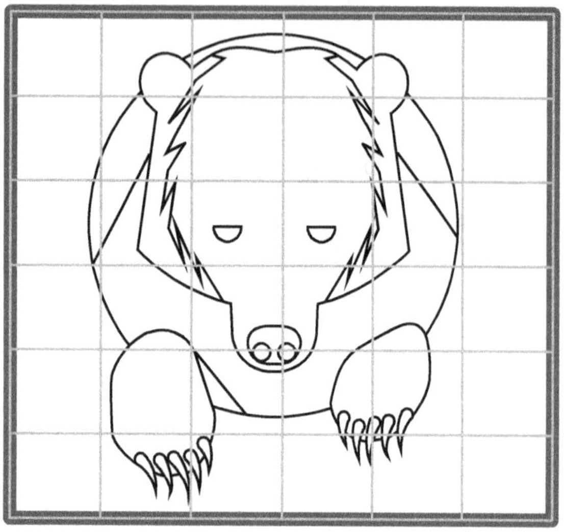

# DRAW
## THE IMAGE

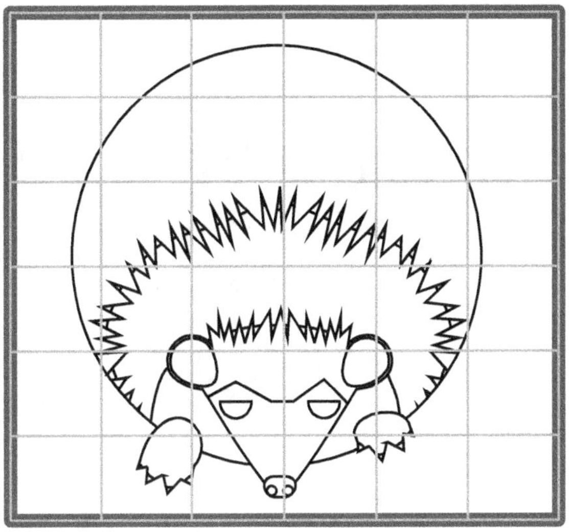

# DRAW THE IMAGE

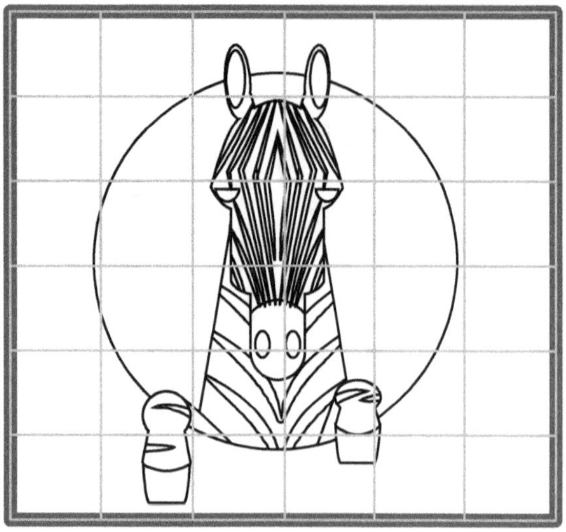

# DRAW THE IMAGE

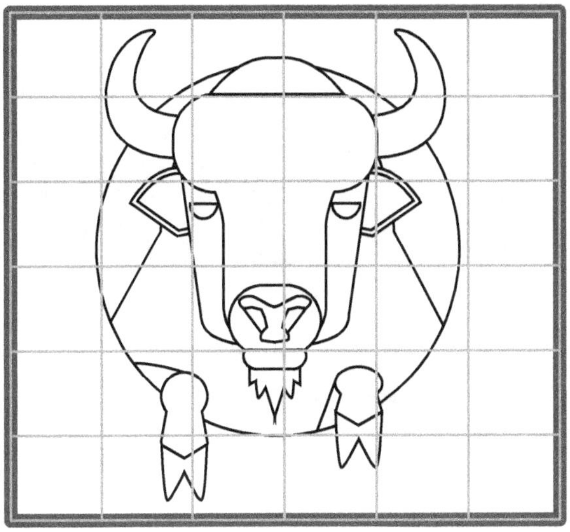

# DRAW
## THE IMAGE

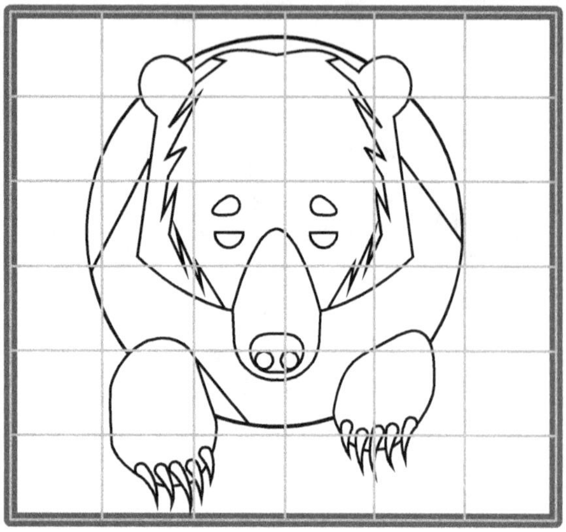

# DRAW THE IMAGE

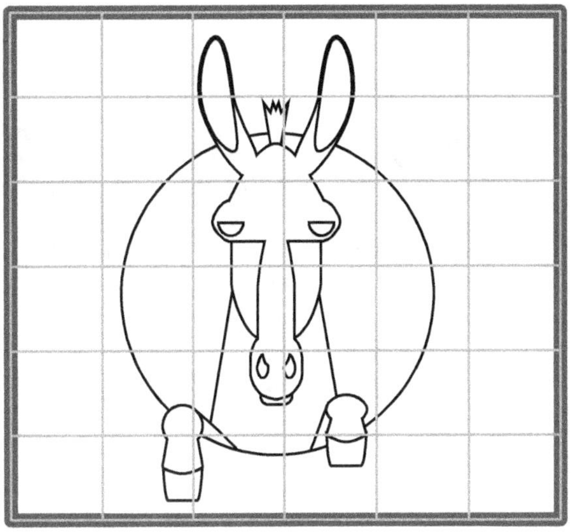

# DRAW THE IMAGE

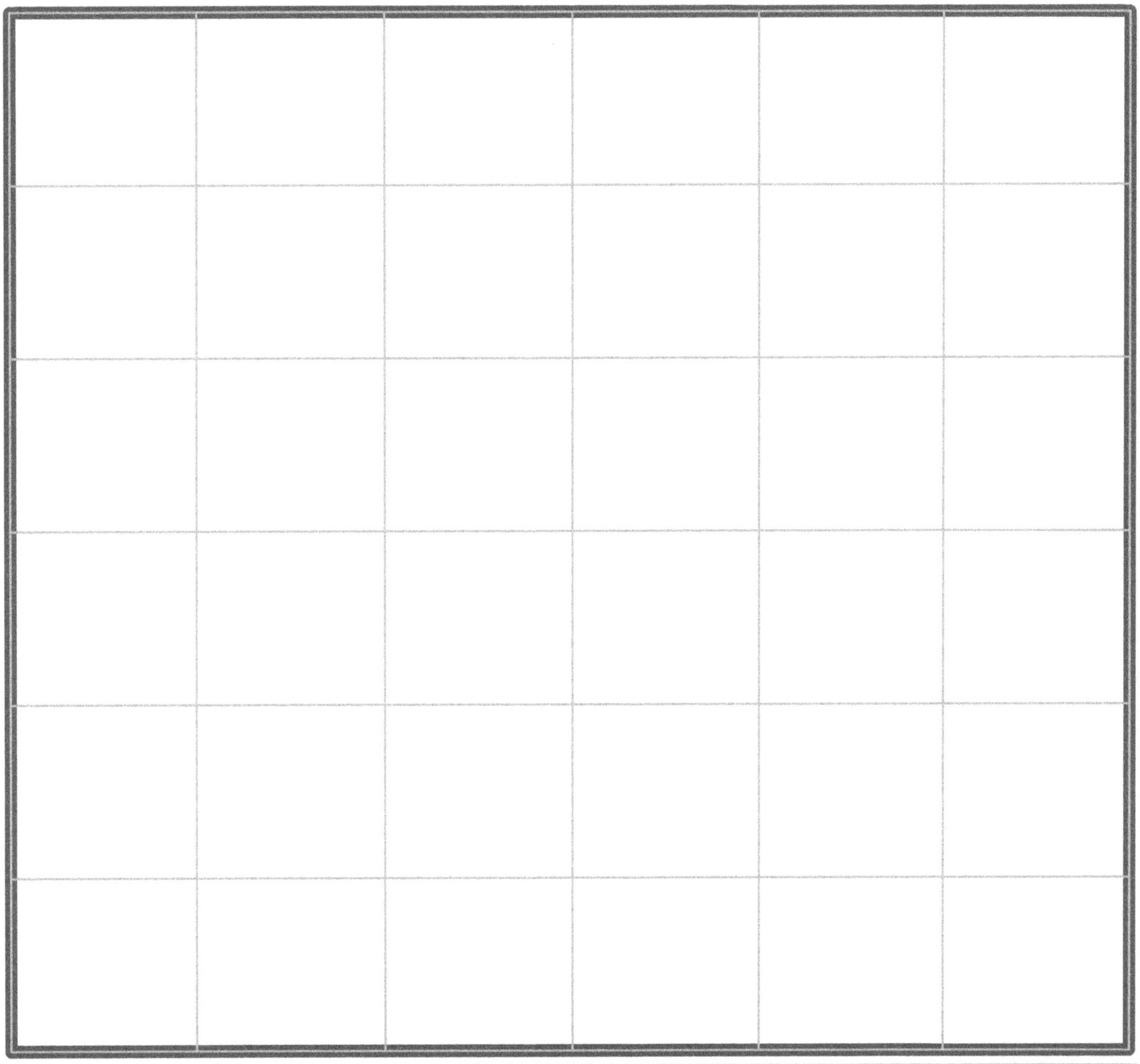

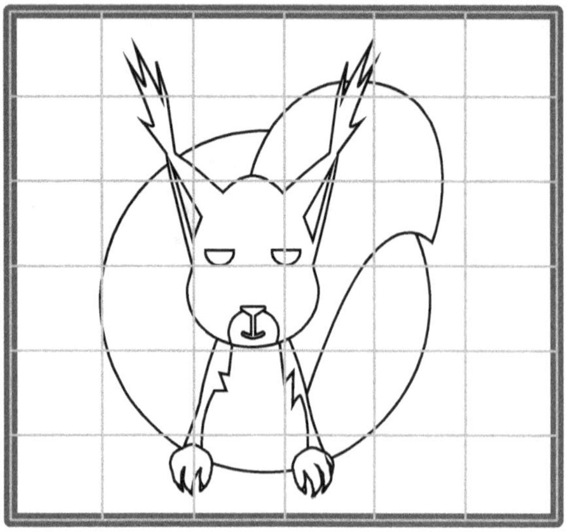

# DRAW THE IMAGE

# DRAW THE IMAGE

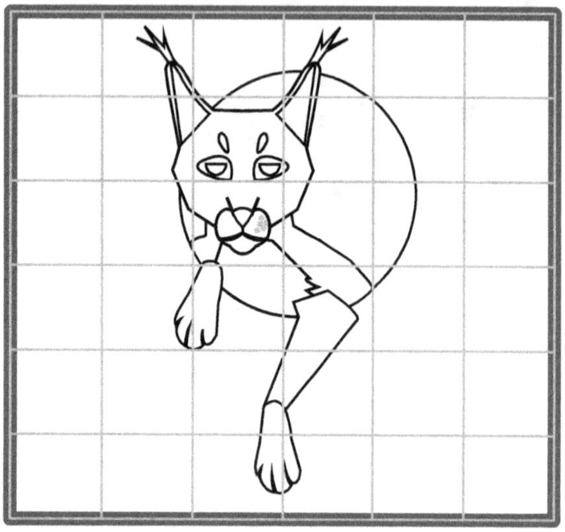

# DRAW
## THE
## IMAGE

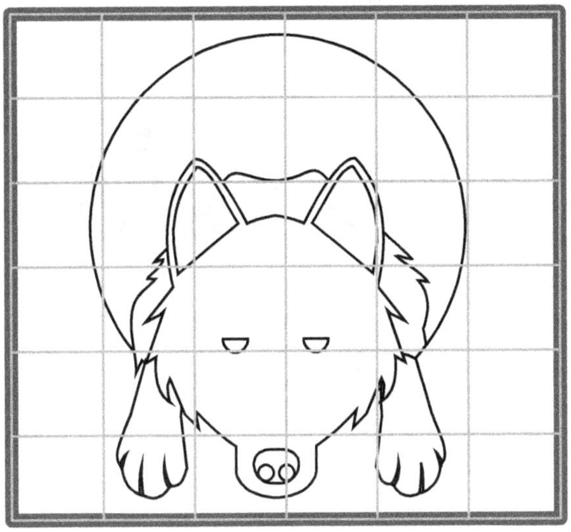

# DRAW
## THE IMAGE

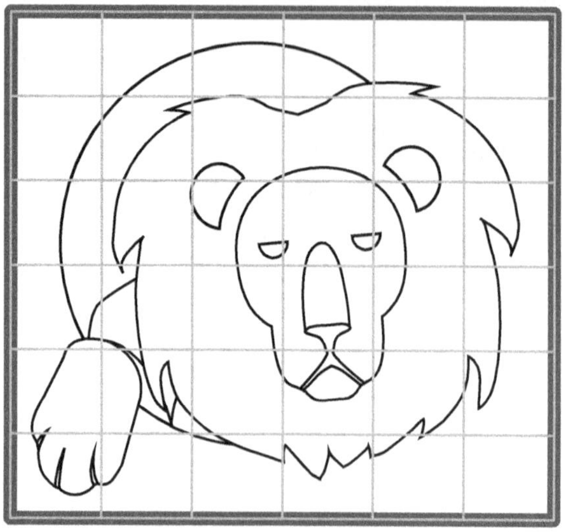

# DRAW THE IMAGE

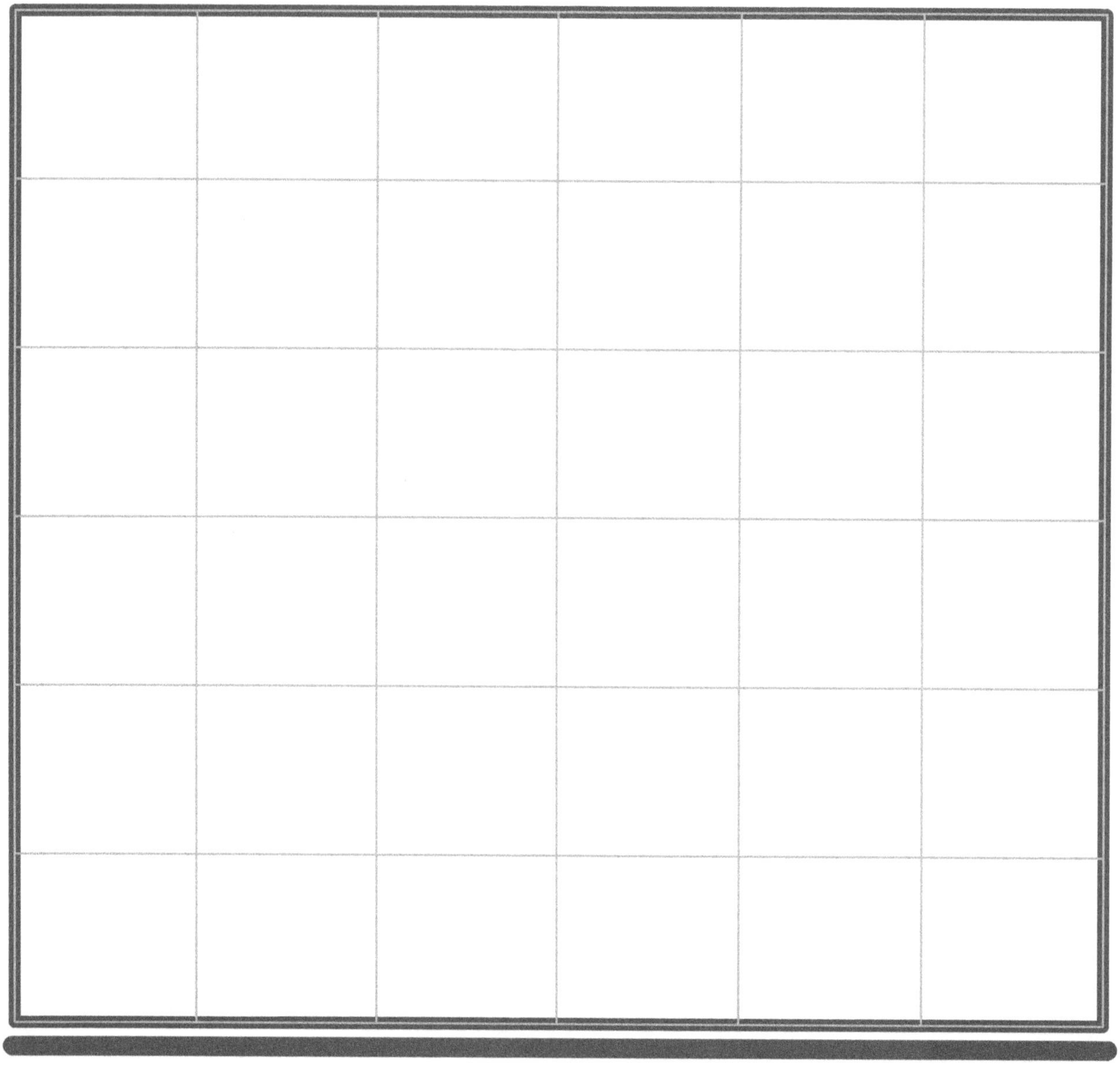

# DRAW THE IMAGE

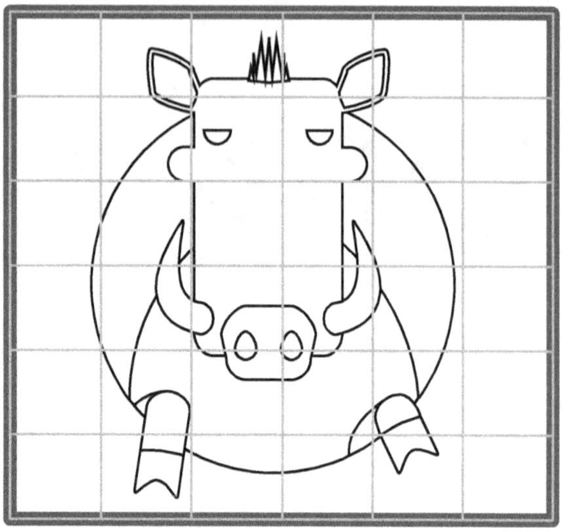

# DRAW THE IMAGE

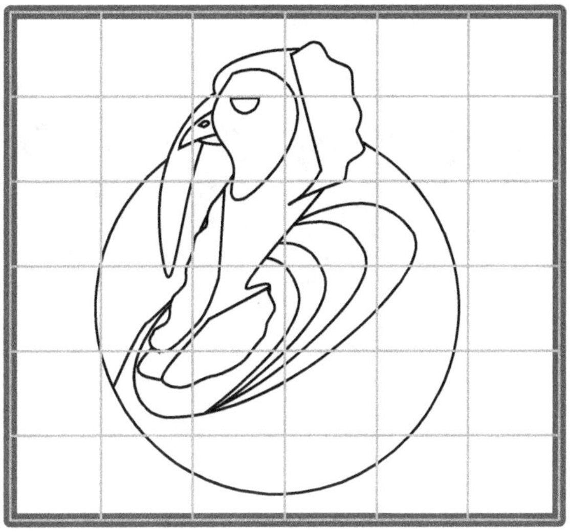

# DRAW
## THE IMAGE

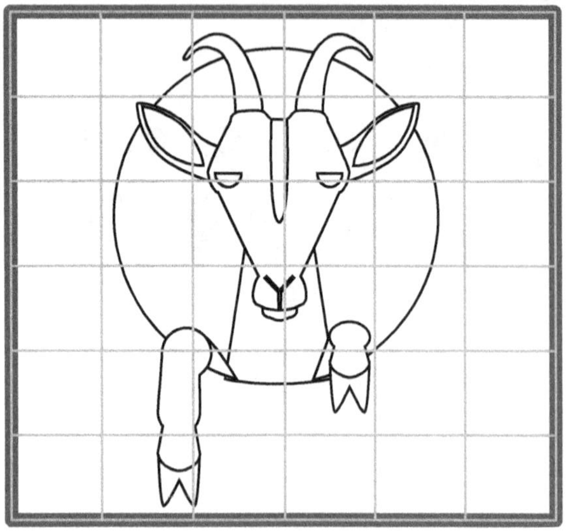

# DRAW THE IMAGE

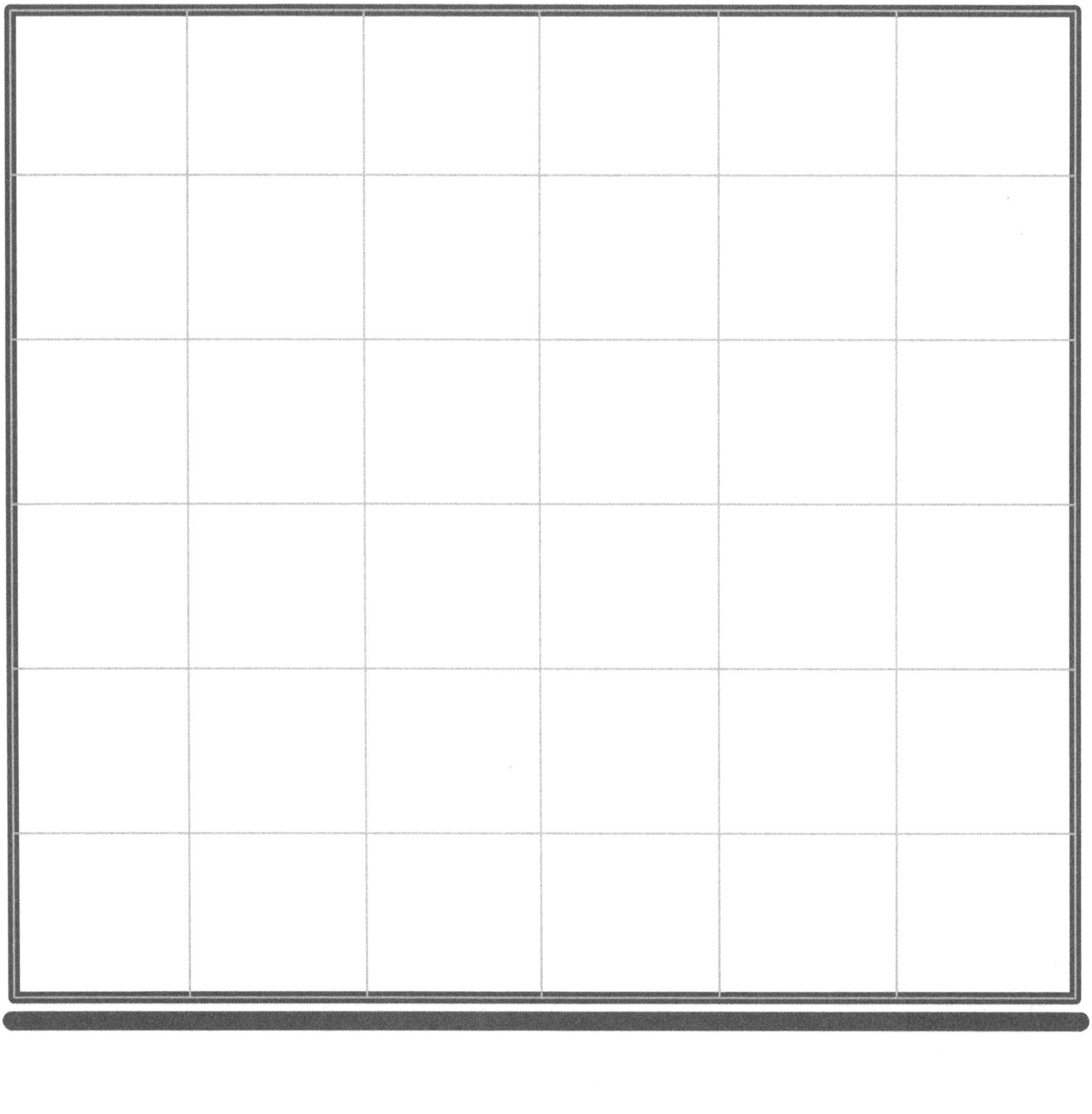

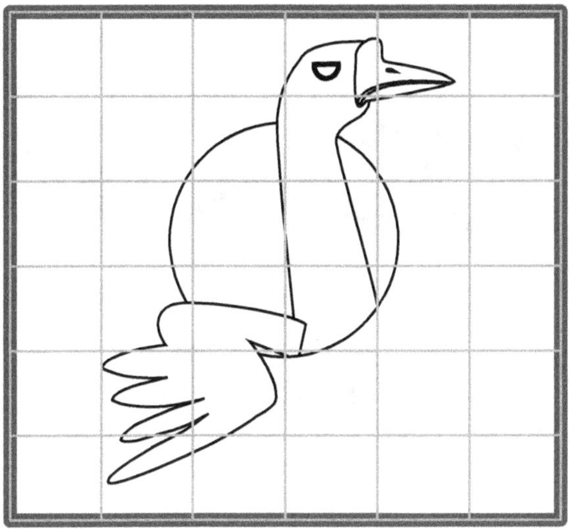

# DRAW THE IMAGE

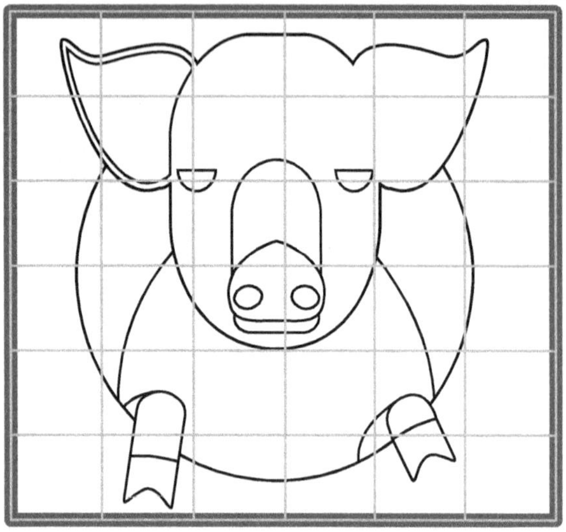

# DRAW
## THE IMAGE

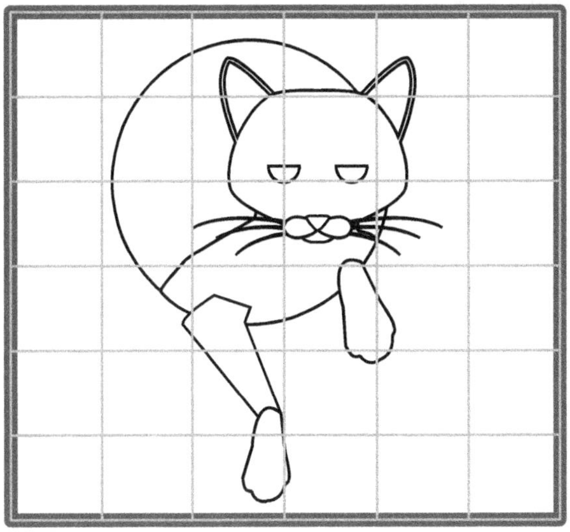

# DRAW THE IMAGE

www.ingramcontent.com/pod-product-compliance
Lightning Source LLC
LaVergne TN
LVHW082323080426
835508LV00042B/1523
*9781683214380*